yes or no?

house

1 Can you see a house?
2 Is the house red?
3 Can you see a door?
4 Is the door green?
5 Has the house got a roof?
6 Is the roof red?
7 Can you see smoke?
8 Can you see six windows?
9 Do you live in a house?
10 Is the door yellow?

numbers

1 2 3 4 5

one   two   three   four   five

1 One and one makes —— .
2 Two and three makes —— .
3 Two and two makes —— .
4 One and three makes —— .
5 Four and one makes —— .

colours

red   green   yellow   blue   black

1 ■ This is —— .
2 ■ This is —— .
3 ■ This is —— .
4 ■ This is —— .
5 ■ This is —— .

dots

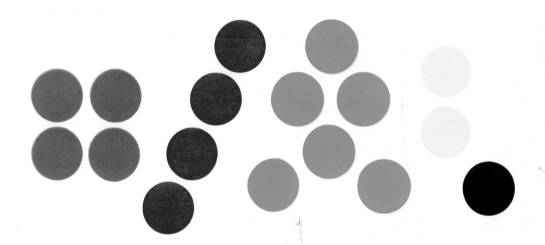

1 How many red dots can you see?
2 Can you see six green dots?
3 How many black dots can you see?
4 How many yellow dots can you see?
5 Can you see four blue dots?

legs

1 A cow has —— legs.
2 A man has —— legs.
3 A dog has —— legs.
4 A bird has —— legs.
5 A pig has —— legs.

how many?

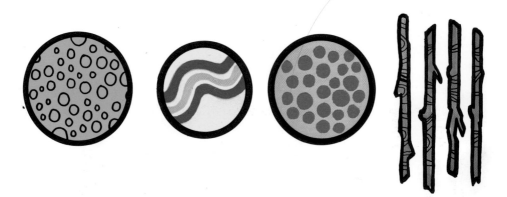

1	How many balls can you see?
2	How many sticks can you see?
3	How many trees can you see?
4	How many dots can you see?
5	How many flowers can you see?

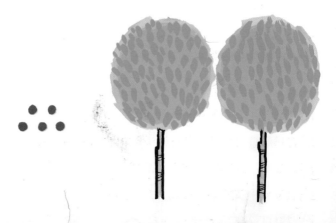

cow

1 How many cows can you see?
2 Is the cow black and white?
3 Do cows eat grass?
4 Is the grass green?
5 Do we get milk from cows?
6 Has a cow got five ears?
7 Has a cow got a tail?
8 Can a cow run?

cow   star

tent

ball

1 I am yellow.
You see me in the sky.
I am small.
I am a —— .

2 I have four legs.
I give milk.
I say moo moo.
I am a —— .

3 I am like a house.
I fold up.
You camp in me.
I am a —— .

4 I am round.
I go up and down.
You play with me.
You hit me with a bat.
I am a —— .

1 Can you see a butterfly?
2 How many birds can you see?
3 Can a flower fly?
4 Has a bird got two wings?
5 How many wings has a butterfly?
6 What colour is the butterfly?
7 What colour is the bird?
8 What colour is the flower?
9 How many petals has the flower?
10 Can a butterfly land on a flower?
11 Can a bird land on a tree?
12 Is the middle of the flower yellow?

butterfly

bird

flower

house grass
bird milk

1 I am red.
I have a door.
I have four windows.
I am a ——— .

2 I am green.
Cows eat me.
Horses eat me.
I am ——— .

3 I come from a cow.
I go in a bottle.
You drink me.
I am ——— .

4 I have wings.
I fly in the sky.
I live in a nest.
I am a ——— .

ducks  pig

1. How many rabbits can you see?
2. Can you see two red fish?
3. Do pigs have tails?
4. Can a rabbit swim?
5. Has a fish got legs?
6. Can ducks swim?
7. Can you see a yellow fish?
8. How many ducks can you see?
9. Do rabbits have long ears?
10. Can you see six fish?

rabbits

fish

wall

cats

1 How many cats are sitting on the wall?
2 How many cats are not sitting on the wall?
3 How many tails can you see?
4 Have all the cats got tails?
5 Is the wall made of wood?
6 Is the wall made of brick?
7 How many ears can you see?
8 What colour are the cats?
9 What colour is the wall?
10 How many cats can you see?

1 Can you see a bird's nest?
2 What is in the nest?
3 Is the nest made of twigs?
4 How many birds can you see?
5 Has a bird got two legs?
6 What colour are the eggs?
7 Can birds fly in the sky?
8 Can you fly in the sky?
9 What colour is the bird?
10 Has the bird got two feet?

nest

bird

foot   bat
nest
gun

1 You play with me.
I am made of wood.
I hit a ball.
I am a ——.

2 You stand on me.
I am at the end of a leg.
I have five toes.
I am a ——.

3 I am made of twigs.
Eggs lie in me.
Birds live in me.
I am a ——.

4 Cowboys have me.
I shoot.
I say bang bang.
I am a ——.

1 How many birds can you see?
2 Is the fence black?
3 Are the birds black?
4 How many trees can you see?
5 What colour is the haystack?
6 How many things are green?
7 Can birds fly?
8 How many things are yellow?
9 Can a tree run?
10 Can a haystack jump?

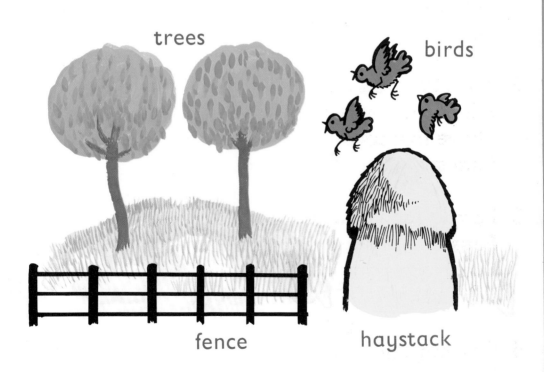

trees

birds

fence

haystack

three doll's prams

front   middle   back

1 How many prams can you see?
2 How many wheels can you see?
3 Can you see a green pram?
4 Can you see a black pram?
5 Can you see six black wheels?
6 Is the red pram in front?
7 Is the yellow pram at the back?
8 Is the green pram in the middle?
9 Can you see two wheels on the pram at the front?
10 How many wheels can you see on the pram in the middle?

1 Can you see a red egg-cup?
2 Can you see two yellow egg-cups?
3 Can you see a red egg-cup with an egg in it?
4 How many egg-cups have eggs in them?
5 Can you see one green egg-cup?
6 How many eggs are not in egg-cups?
7 Do you like to eat eggs?
8 How many egg-cups do not have eggs in them?
9 Is the middle of an egg yellow?
10 How many eggs can you see altogether?

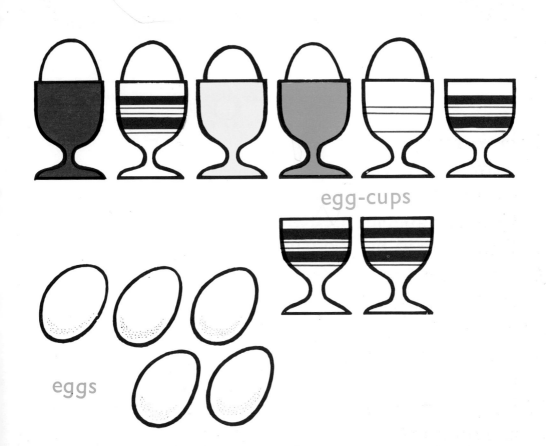

egg-cups

eggs

hens

1 How many hens can you see?
2 Is the yellow hen eating grass?
3 Are the red hens eating grass?
4 Is the yellow hen in the middle?
5 Can you see three red hens?
6 Do we get eggs from hens?
7 Do you like hens?
8 Are all the hens eating?
9 Can a hen run?
10 How many legs has a hen?